The Dino-Sphere

When Birds Had Teeth

by Ruth Owen

Consultant:
Dougal Dixon, Paleontologist
Member of the Society of Vertebrate Paleontology
United Kingdom

BEARPORT PUBLISHING

New York, New York

Credits
Cover, © Herschel Hoffmeyer/Shutterstock; 2–3, © Warpaint/Shutterstock; 4–5, © Herschel Hoffmeyer and © Kirbyzz/Shutterstock; 6, © Herschel Hoffmeyer/Shutterstock and © Catmando/Shutterstock; 7T, © MikhailSh/Shutterstock; 7B, © Marcin Perkowski/Shutterstock; 8, © Herschel Hoffmeyer/Shutterstock; 9T, © John Sibbick/Science Photo Library; 9B, © Zach Tirrell/Creative Commons; 10TL, © Phil Degginger/Carnegie Museum/Alamy; 10TR, © Gabbro/Alamy; 10B, © H. Zell/Creative Commons; 11, © James Kuether; 12, © Jaime Chirinos/Science Photo Library; 13, © Zheng et al; 14–15, © Kostyantyn Ivanyshen/Shutterstock; 15R, © Daderot/Creative Commons; 16, © Mohamad Haghani/Alamy and © Dmitry Naumov/Shutterstock; 17, © O. Louis Mazzatenta/Getty Images; 18, © solarseven/Shutterstock; 19, © Phillip Krzeminski; 20, © Roger Clark ARPS/Shutterstock; 21L, © Super Prin/Shutterstock; 21BL, © Stockphoto mania/Shutterstock; 21BR, © Narupon Nimpaiboon/Shutterstock; 21R, © buteo/Shutterstock; 22T, © Andrea Danti/Shutterstock; 22C, © Elenarts/Shutterstock and © Phil West/Shutterstock; 22B, © Nor Gal/Shutterstock; 23T, © SABPICS/Shutterstock; 23C, © Akkharat Jarusilawong/Shutterstock; 23B, © Linda Bucklin/Shutterstock.

Publisher: Kenn Goin
Senior Editor: Joyce Tavolacci
Creative Director: Spencer Brinker
Image Researcher: Ruth Owen Books

Library of Congress Cataloging-in-Publication Data

Names: Owen, Ruth, 1967– author.
Title: When birds had teeth / by Ruth Owen.
Description: New York, New York : Bearport Publishing, [2019] | Series: The dino-sphere | Includes bibliographical references and index.
Identifiers: LCCN 2018053521 (print) | LCCN 2018055216 (ebook) | ISBN 9781642802573 (Ebook) | ISBN 9781642801880 (library) | ISBN 978-1-64280-840-7 (pbk.)
Subjects: LCSH: Dinosaurs—Flight—Juvenile literature. | Birds, Fossil—Juvenile literature. | Birds—Evolution—Juvenile literature.
Classification: LCC QE861.6.F45 (ebook) | LCC QE861.6.F45 O94 2019 (print) | DDC 567.918—dc23
LC record available at https://lccn.loc.gov/2018053521

For more information, write to Bearport Publishing, 5357 Penn Avenue South, Minneapolis MN 55419.
Printed in the United States of America.

Contents

Crunch Time! 4
A Bird with Teeth 6
Bird or Dinosaur? 8
An Amazing Discovery 10
Lots of Birds 12
Tiny Wings 14
Beaked Bird 16
Asteroid Strike! 18
Thousands of Birds 20

Glossary 22
Index 24
Read More 24
Learn More Online 24
About the Author 24

Crunch Time!

A hungry bird grabs a dragonfly in its jaws.

Crunch! It bites the insect with its sharp teeth.

The bird is called *Archaeopteryx*.

It lived 150 million years ago in the time of the dinosaurs!

The name *Archaeopteryx* means "old wing."

Archaeopteryx
(ahr-kee-OP-tuh-riks)

A Bird with Teeth

Scientists discovered *Archaeopteryx* **fossils** in 1861.

The **prehistoric** bird was the size of a large crow.

It had three clawed fingers on each wing.

It also had sharp teeth and a long, bony tail.

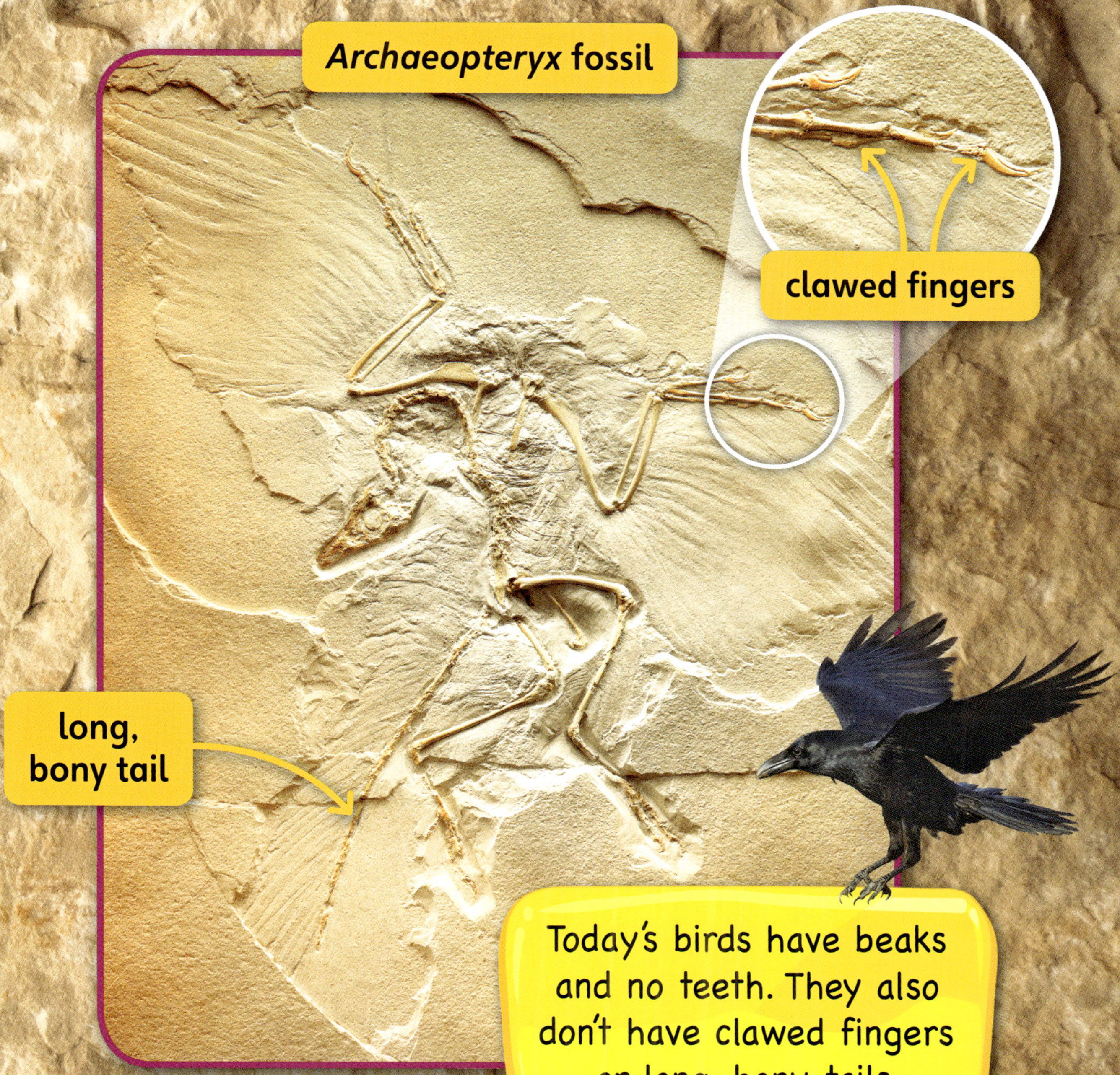

Today's birds have beaks and no teeth. They also don't have clawed fingers or long, bony tails.

Bird or Dinosaur?

With its teeth and claws, *Archaeopteryx* looked like a dinosaur.

Yet, it also had feathers and could fly.

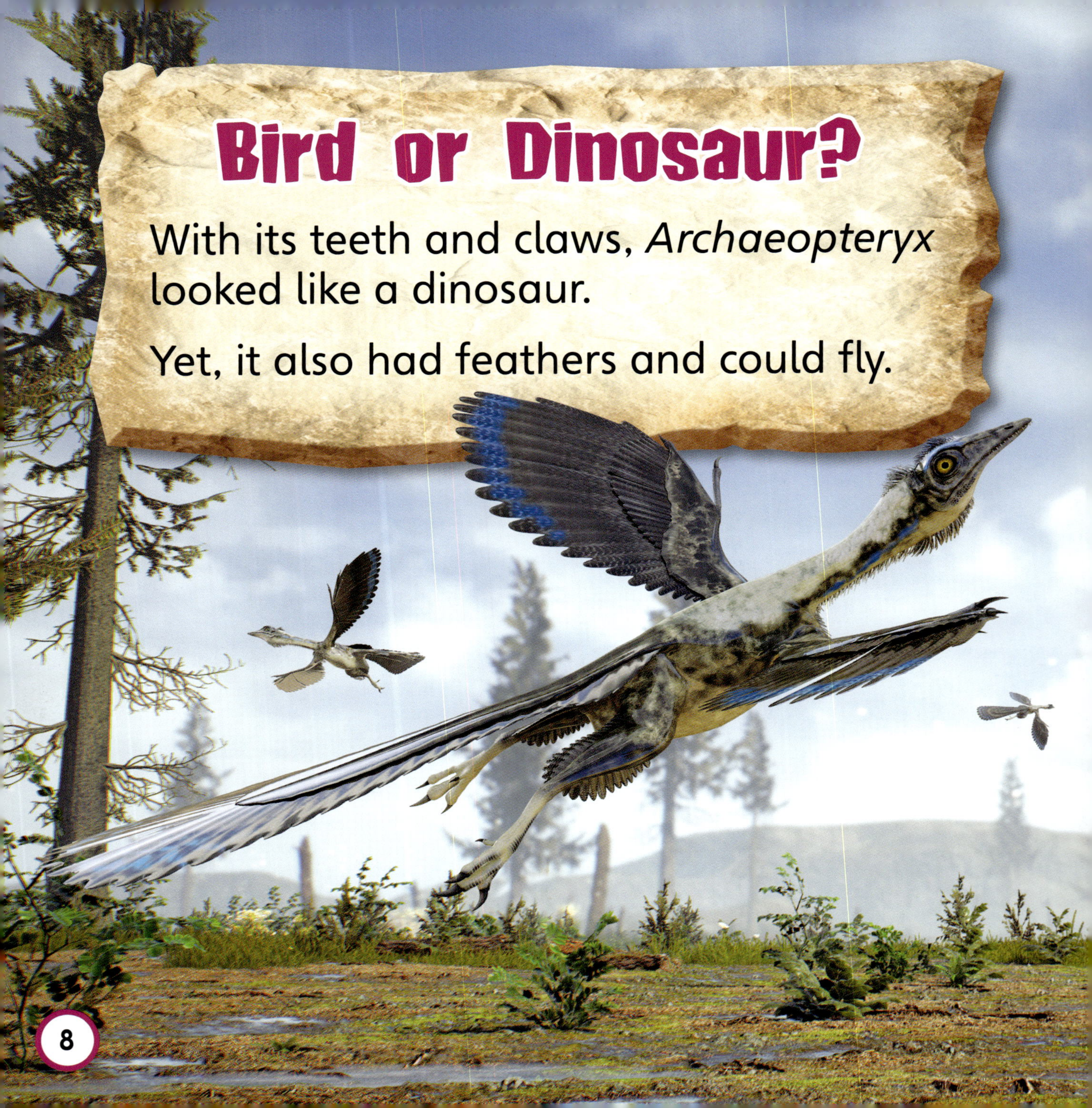

So why did this creature resemble a dinosaur?

The fossils of *Archaeopteryx* and a dinosaur called *Compsognathus* look a lot alike.

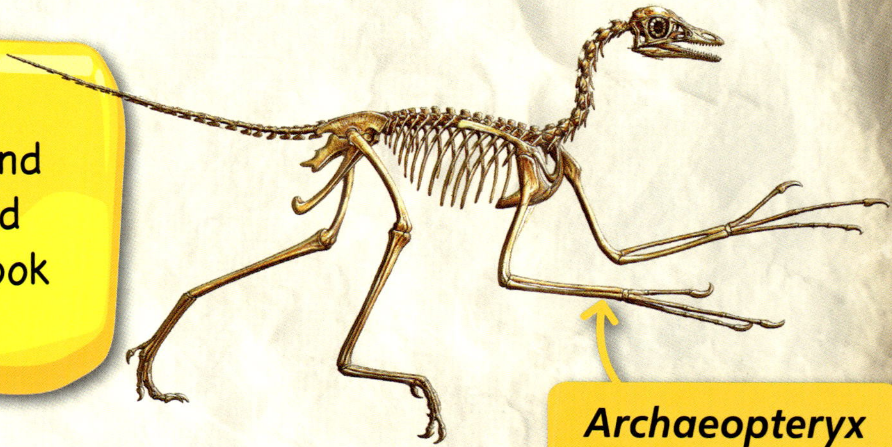

***Archaeopteryx* skeleton**

***Compsognathus* skeleton**

***Compsognathus* (komp-sog-NATH-uhs)**

An Amazing Discovery

Scientists studied lots of fossils and made an amazing discovery.

Birds came from dinosaurs!

dinosaur skull fossil

dinosaur foot fossil

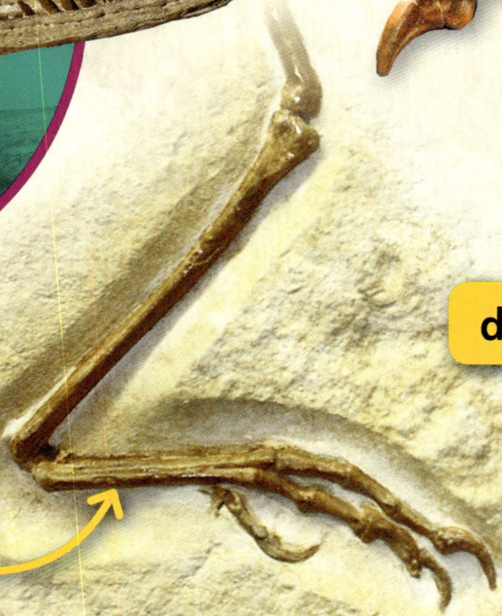

bird foot fossil

The dinosaurs that became birds walked on two legs.

They were related to dinosaurs called *Velociraptors*.

The dinosaurs that became birds **evolved** over millions of years.

Lots of Birds

Some prehistoric birds could fly, while others were **flightless**.

Patagopteryx were flightless birds. Scientists think they probably lived in large flocks.

Yanornis was a chicken-sized bird that could fly.

Scientists think its main food was fish. Why?

They found a fossilized *Yanornis* filled with fish!

Tiny Wings

A bird called *Caudipteryx* lived in China.

This peacock-sized bird had tiny wings and couldn't fly.

Like some modern birds, *Caudipteryx* ate small stones.

The stones helped to grind up seeds and other food in its stomach.

Scientists found stones in the stomach of a fossilized *Caudipteryx*.

Beaked Bird

Confuciusornis was the size of a pigeon.

It lived 120 million years ago, but it looked a lot like a modern bird.

Scientists think *Confuciusornis* was one of the first birds to have a toothless beak.

Instead of a bony tail, it had two long tail feathers.

Confuciusornis was able to fly. Scientists can tell this by looking at its bones and feathers.

Asteroid Strike!

What happened to the prehistoric birds?

About 66 million years ago, a giant **asteroid** struck Earth.

The asteroid caused fires and floods.

Most of the prehistoric birds became **extinct**.

Most dinosaurs also went extinct after the asteroid strike.

Thousands of Birds

Some kinds of prehistoric birds survived the asteroid strike.

They evolved over millions of years.

Eventually, they became penguins, parrots, and other birds.

Today, there are 10,000 different kinds of birds on Earth!

All the birds on Earth today are related to dinosaurs—but none have teeth!

Glossary

asteroid (AS-ter-royd) a large rock traveling through space

evolved (ih-VOLVD) changed gradually over a long period of time

extinct (ek-STINGKT) gone forever

flightless (FLAHYT-lis)
unable to fly

fossils (FOSS-uhlz)
the rocky remains of animals and plants that lived millions of years ago

prehistoric (pree-hi-STAWR-ik)
a time long ago before humans lived on Earth

Index

Archaeopteryx 4–5, 6–7, 8–9
asteroids 18–19, 20
beaks 7, 16–17
Caudipteryx 14–15
Compsognathus 9
Confuciusornis 16–17
dinosaurs 4, 8–9, 10–11, 19
fossils 6–7, 9, 10, 13, 15, 17
Patagopteryx 12
tails 6–7, 17
teeth 4, 6–7, 8, 17, 21
Velociraptor 11
wings 4, 6–7, 14
Yanornis 13

Read More

Rissman, Rebecca. *Velociraptor and Other Raptors (The Need-to-Know Facts)*. North Mankato, MN: Capstone (2016).

Shone, Rob. *Archaeopteryx: The First Bird (Graphic Dinosaurs)*. New York: Rosen (2012).

Learn More Online

To learn more about prehistoric birds, visit
www.bearportpublishing.com/dinosphere

About the Author

Ruth Owen has been developing and writing children's books for more than ten years. She first discovered dinosaurs when she was four years old—and loves them as much today as she did then!